First Poems for Thinking

ROBERT FISHER

Nash Pollock Publishing

© 2000 Robert Fisher

First published in 2000 by
Nash Pollock Publishing
32 Warwick Street
Oxford OX4 1SX

9 8 7

Orders to:
York Publishing Services
64 Hallfield Road
Layerthorpe
York YO31 7ZQ

A catalogue record of this book is available from the British
Library.

ISBN 1 898255 30 X

Design, typesetting and production management by
Black Dog Design, Buckingham

Printed and bound by The Cromwell Press, Great Britain, Trowbrige, Wiltshire.

Contents

Introduction

All poetry is magic. It is a spell against insensitivity, failure of imagination, ignorance and barbarism. The way that a good poem 'works' on a reader is as mysterious and hard to explain as the possible working of a charm or spell. A poem is much more than a mere arrangement of words on paper, or the tongue. Its hints, suggestions, the echoes it sets off in the mind ... all join up with the reader's thoughts and feelings and make a kind of magical union – Charles Causley

A poem is alive, because it says things when you read it – Tom, aged six

The first principle for sharing poems with young children is to use poems that you and they enjoy. *First Poems for Thinking* contains more than thirty poems that I have enjoyed sharing with young children. These poems, both traditional and contemporary, are drawn from a variety of cultures and traditions.

The poems chosen are written to communicate something of importance, and are therefore poems for thinking. They are for children to enjoy, but also to challenge them. Each of the poems is followed by a discussion plan of questions to extend children's thinking about the poem. There is also a discussion plan that raises questions about one theme or key concept explored in the poem. Follow-up activities are suggested to encourage children to extend their thinking and their response to poems. The book also contains a glossary of terms used in discussing poetry.

The poems and discussion plans can be used in a variety of ways, for example as a stimulus for thinking with:

* Individual children
* children working in pairs
* small groups within a class
* the whole class as a community of enquiry
* larger groups of children, such as a school assembly.

This book focuses on ways of fostering a love of poetry through a range of poems, and on ways to enable children to become thoughtful readers who are able to pose questions, to discuss and to evaluate critically the texts they read through questions, discussion, reflective writing, art, drama and other activities that help develop thinking and the use of poetry across the curriculum. The belief that underlies this book is that both enjoyment and understanding are essential if children are to gain most from their experience of poetry. Or as Katie, aged seven, said, 'When you hear a poem you don't always get it, but when you talk about it it helps.'

Poetry and the young child

Every child is born with the ability to respond to words and ideas in a playful way. From the first rhythmic words such as 'da-da-da-da' or 'ma-ma' the young child responds and revels in syllabic rhythm. The young child's babbling speech is an early expression of their poetic voice, playing with sounds. Later they will use words to play with ideas, as when a three year old said: 'Look, the tree is snowing leaves.'

Poetry begins with a fascination for words, with enjoyment of word games, for example with rhyming words, such as the following strung together by four year olds: 'sad dad had a bad lad', 'may play today stay', and 'a vet in a jet set met a wet pet'. This early experience of rhymes and rhythms needs to be extended to an enjoyment of poems.

What a young child needs is a rich range of poetry books to read and to be read to. Hearing particular poems and rhymes a number of times will help them internalise the words and sounds, and they will begin spontaneously to memorise their favourite rhymes. What parents and teachers can do is to help children both to hear and to understand poems. They can explain what to expect from a poem or poetry book, help them through questioning and discussion to make meaning from poems, and show them how they too can communicate through poetry and create their own poems.

But what is a poem?

According to James, aged six, a poem 'is a kind of picture in words'. A poem is both sounds in the air as well as words pictured on a page. It takes time to absorb a poem, to explore the world it creates, its language, its sounds and the message or story it conveys. Dylan Thomas once said poetry 'makes you laugh, cry, prickle, be silent, makes your toenails twinkle.' Poems can serve many purposes. The purposes of poetry are wider than any other kind of writing: they can be used to tell stories, play games with language, record experience, or reflect thoughts and feelings. A poem might be about the real world, or an invented world of the imagination, or both. A poem can transform the ordinary into the extraordinary. It can give voice to an inner world of dreams and imaginings. Like philosophy, poetry often begins in wonder about the world, and the ways in which words can reflect, distort and transform the world.

Every poem is about something, and uses words in a special way. It uses 'the best words in the best order' as Coleridge said, to tell its story.

How do we help children respond to poetry? A poem may lead to many kinds of thoughts, feelings and ideas. There is no one way to experience or appreciate a poem, but many ways. We will now explore some ways of using poems to help a young child to enjoy poetry, to understand poetry, and to develop their reading skills.

Ways of working with a poem	Roles of the child	Key questions
• Speaking and Listening		
• Reading	Code-breaker	*What does it say?*
• Questioning		
• Discussing	Meaning maker	*What does it mean?*
• Expressing	Reading-responder	*What does it mean to me?*
• Composing	Reading-user	*What can we do with it?*

Speaking and listening

Poetry is made for speaking. The earliest poetry was spoken or sung. The first poems that children hear are often the half-remembered nursery rhymes recited to them by parents. These early rhymes may be much repeated, and there is good reason for this. According to the poet W H Auden, what makes a poem special is that it is 'memorable speech'. A poem lays down a track in the memory that can be travelled over again and again, so that language becomes embedded in experience. The words and phrases of a much-loved poem or nursery rhyme become not merely items of knowledge, but are given life and meaning by being embedded in an original poem which becomes part of us when laid down in long term memory. Learning by heart in the natural way,

through repeated speaking and listening, connects the child to a literary inheritance. When they share the words and thoughts of a poem, they are given a poetic voice through which to speak, and words which will echo in the memory. Later, having listened to and expressed the voices of others, they will come to create poetry using their own words and ideas.

We begin by listening. Poetry feeds the ear. Lucky the child who has poetry read to them each week by a parent or teacher. Some teachers try to read a poem a day to their class, with maybe a 'favourite poem' session on Friday. Children can also be encouraged to listen on their own or with others to poetry tapes. Listening to poems can become a regular part of classroom activity. A section of the classroom can be turned into a Listening Corner, with a ready supply of tapes. Children can record their favourites and listen to poems recorded by others. Teachers or parents can create their own tapes of spoken poetry to share with children.

In preparing to share poetry with children it is a good idea to practise reading the poem(s) to yourself first. Try to add part of yourself to the reading, through emphasising key words, adding humour or passion to your favourite bits. Even better if the child has the words or book to follow or read as they listen. Encourage your children to read or recite favourite poems to each other. Ultimately the aim is to teach children to read to themselves. To want to read poetry they must first have enjoyed hearing poetry spoken to them. They must have savoured the sounds of poems, and enjoyed entering into other people's minds. The initial sharing of a poem could involve many kinds of speaking, for example whisper, chant, slow or fast reading, or reading with added sound effects. A good poem has its own musical voice, and the voice is the musical instrument through which the poem is expressed. No wonder Carlyle defined poetry as 'musical thoughts'.

Children should not only listen to the music of poetry, they should speak poetry regularly. After your first reading of a poem, children can be encouraged to 'read along' with you. This may simply mean asking them to repeat words in the poem they remember. These will often be rhyming words. Learning to say poetry is as important as learning to hear it. Invite a child to say a word or line for you during the re-reading. A different child's voice could be used for each line, or they could be encouraged to repeat parts of the poem in pairs or groups. The sequence used in presenting a poem to children might include:

- practice in reading the poem to yourself (perhaps tape this for the child to hear later)
- showing the children what the poem looks like (the words on a page)
- reading the poem to the children (repeating this if necessary)
- inviting children to read or say parts of the poem with you
- encouraging them to say the poem in pairs, or as a group.

Children can be invited to call out the rhyming words of simple poems, for example the rhymes in the following limerick:

> There was a young man from Dunoon,
> Who always ate soup with a ...
> He said, 'As I eat
> Neither fish, fowl or ... ,
> I should finish my dinner quite ...

Young children often find little difficulty in supplying the rhymes 'Dunoon/spoon/soon', and 'eat/meat'. What does surprise children is that the missing words in this poem are 'fork', 'flesh' and 'quick'. This shows that you need not be restricted to given rhyme patterns, but can create interesting effects by supplying your own, possibly bizarre, rhyming words. In this way rhyming poetry can be an ideal means for developing children's phonic skills.

It is a shame however if children are limited to a diet of sing-song rhymes. They need to hear a rich repertoire of different kinds of poems, including poems written in sprung rhythm or free verse. Poems need not simply be spoken, but can be enlivened by other 'expressive' means, including hand movements and actions, the use of puppets, musical instruments and so on (for more on creative ways of performing poetry see 'Expressing' below). A question to ask yourself before you present a poem to children is 'How can I add interest to my reading?' It may be through use of voice or gesture that added colour is given to a spoken poem. One infant teacher describes her own approach thus: 'I try my best to memorise the poem beforehand so I can give my children full attention while 'reading' it to them. This adds to the drama of the situation both for them and me!'

Reading

A poem is encoded in language. Helping children to crack the code, to be able to read the word and so release the poem from the page, is a challenging task. This means helping young children focus on the sounds of words, but also focusing on what words mean. The importance of reading to young children has been emphasised in many studies, as has the value of learning nursery rhymes and other kinds of word play. Studies show that young children's sensitivity to rhyme is particularly important in later success in reading. That is why singing and chanting rhymes can be so important in developing early literacy.

Reading aloud to children has a positive effect on developing early reading ability, through helping children to differentiate and recognise different sounds (phonemes) in words, but so does getting children to see the words as you read to them. There is a problem in sharing normal-sized books with large groups of children, hence the use of 'big books' in teaching literacy in schools. Of course you do not need big books, nor coloured pictures, to teach literacy. Indeed many of the 'big books' used in schools today are of poor literary quality and the illustrations may encourage teachers and children to rely too much on gaining meaning from simple picture images. A poem is a text made up of words: it does not involve pictures on the page but encourages pictures in the mind. It is better if possible to rely on text alone, since this forces the child to engage in decoding the words, not rely on picture cues. It also encourages the creation of images in the child's mind. If you want a group of children to share the words of a poem then you can simply print them in bold lower case letters on a large sheet of paper for all to see.

The following is a summary of key principles in sharing the reading of poetry with young children:

- Choose poems to share which you and the children will like.
- Present the poem with whole-hearted enjoyment.
- Repeat the reading for children to gain more from the poem.
- Involve the children if possible in the reading eg by chanting or putting actions to the words.
- Extend the reading with discussion and further activities about the poem.

Young children find poetry easier to read if it is rhythmic, and rhymes help the text to be predictable. Nursery rhymes and the kinds of 'kids' verse' that are their modern equivalents, such as the Dr Seuss books, help develop phonemic awareness. The trouble is that if phonic or rhyming content is all a teacher is after then any piece of doggerel will do. As one child said of poems after listening to a nonsense rhyme, 'I like the way they sound but they don't mean anything.' Another young child said when his teacher was beginning a familiar rhyme, 'I know the tune of that' but the tune for that child had no meaning.

Children should be engaged in trying to understand the meaning of poems as well as enjoying the sound they make. After all, it is the meanings that you derive from a poem that gives it its significance. Children should be engaged in seeking meaning from a wide variety of poems. Reading poetry with children can be a significant source of growth in vocabulary and com- prehension if it is followed up questioning and discussion. As Nikki, aged five, says, 'Sometimes you have to talk what the words mean.'

Questioning

After reading the poem two or three times, begin the discussion by asking some questions. Most young children do not know that a poem is there to be questioned until they are shown how. The function of questions is to focus attention on the poem and engage the mind in trying to make meaning from the poem. If we want them to read for meaning the general question we want them to answer is *What does it mean?*

This is best done as a follow-up to shared reading. The main purpose of this activity is to encourage children to think hard about what they have read or heard. This questioning of a text as a group is known by many names. Adults engaged in this process might call it a Literary Circle, the Literacy Hour guidelines call it Shared Reading, other teachers refer to it as a Thinking Circle or Community of Enquiry (see below). In this shared activity teachers question children about the text, so that they in turn will learn how to interrogate the text for themselves. This kind of interactive reading is what good readers do. They do not simply read the words in their mind, but are actively engaged in interrogating and making meaning from the text. The questioning we do with children we hope later they will learn to do for themselves. But what kinds of question should we ask?

We might ask children closed or open questions, or a combination of both. Closed questions are those which seek a single answer, for example:

- What is the title of the poem?
- Does it rhyme?
- Who wrote the poem?

Such questions probe knowledge about the poem and are either right or wrong. Open questions probe understanding of the poem and are open to a range of possible answers. The value of such questioning in a group is that children are exposed to a variety of viewpoints. They get to hear ideas they would never have thought of themselves. They learn that many interpretations and opinions are possible, and that differences of view are acceptable if supported by suitable reasons or evidence from the text. It is by open questions that we help to open children's minds.

Open questions that can be asked of any poem include:

- What is the poem about?
- Did you like the poem? Why, or why not?
- Can you pick out a bit you like and tell us why?
- Do you think this is a good poem? Why do, or don't, you think so?
- Is there anything in the poem you don't understand?

Better than questions asked by the teacher will be questions asked by the children themselves. This is because what we are after is self-directed, not just teacher-directed learning. We are not only teaching about a particular poem, we are also showing the child how to question, discuss and evaluate any poem. We are not just helping them to understand this poem, but how to interrogate and make meaning from any text. To do this we need to encourage them to think about, question, and comment on what has been read. One way to encourage them to think about, question, and comment on what has been read is by having a community of enquiry about the poem.

A Community of Enquiry

A community of enquiry is a means of getting children to share, question and discuss a poem in a safe and stimulating environment. It offers the opportunity for children to learn to think for themselves about poetry and to learn from the thinking of others. So how do we create a community of enquiry using Poems for Thinking?

In a typical community of enquiry the teacher will:
- present and read the poem, asking children to think about the poem
- invite their comments or questions about the poem, and write these on the board
- lead a discussion about one or more of the children's questions or comments

- introduce further group or individual activity about the poem
- ask children in a plenary session to review their response to the poem

This is how these elements apply to a Poems for Thinking lesson. After reading and re-reading the poem, ask some questions about the poem (sample questions are given in the discussion plans after each poem), and invite the children to share any of their own thoughts and questions about the poem. Ask for example: 'Is there anything strange, interesting or puzzling about the poem?' Show that you value their comments by recording what they say on the board. Write the name of the child on the board next to their question or comment as a record and a recognition of their contribution. This list of children's comments and questions can then form the agenda for discussion. Ask for example: 'Who can answer Greg's question?' or 'Who agrees or disagrees with Anna's comment?'

The following are some questions asked by a group of six year olds about the poem 'Why?' (see p 70):

- What does 'Why' mean? (William)
- Why does every line begin with 'Why'? (Rosie)
- Why are there so many questions? (Nicola)
- Can't you find all the answers in books? (Paul)
- Doesn't a teacher know? (Sunil)

The teacher then leads a discussion with the class by inviting them to suggest possible answers to each question. During the discussion the teacher also made use of questions from the discussion plan 'Thinking about questions'(p 71) to challenge children's thinking. These questions model the sort of questions she hoped the children will learn to ask for themselves. The children then went into groups to make up their own list of questions which they then shared with others in the plenary session.

What is clear from research into this way of working is that children who are used to asking questions, in a classroom that encourages pupil questioning, will tend to ask more questions, better questions and come to think of reading as a process of active enquiry. Or as Natalie, aged seven, put it, 'When you think about it there is always some question to ask.'

The Literacy Hour and a 'Poems for Thinking' approach share some commom features. Both emphasise the importance disscussing the text to identify themes, ideas, and implicit meanings. Both aim to develop critical and reflective reading, The books in this series (see further reading below) not only emphasise the importance of children formulating their own questions but discuss further ways of involving them in philosophical discussion by creating a community of enquiry in the classroom.

A Literacy Hour can be adapted to benefit from a 'Poems for Thinking' approach, or time may be found for more extended discussion of poems than is allowed in a Literacy Hour. This book aims to be a flexible resource for you to use in ways which suit you and your children. It will develop literacy but is about more than literacy, it is also about teaching children to think, in particular to think philosophically about poems and about themselves and the world. It provides an ideal introduction to poetry but also to philosophical discussion with children.

Discussing

Usually the meaning of a poem is distilled in the fewest words. If children are to understand what Ted Hughes calls the 'spirit' of a poem the child must integrate the meanings of the words, with images and rhythms. In this way they create their own mental model of what the poem describes. For this to happen they need to have some idea of the main point of the poem, and be sensitive to the relationships between the poem's living parts. Because a poem is so concise its meanings are often enigmatic. Inference and deduction are needed to make sense of what is suggested and links between what is said and what is implied. Even the simplest poems create ambiguities. In the nursery rhyme, where exactly were Jack and Jill going? When did it take place? Why were they fetching a pail of water? How did they fall down? What happened then?

Discussion with others can help us to deepen our understanding through the sharing of ideas, creative insights and critical response to the poem. This is not to spoil the mutual enjoyment of the poem, but to enrich that enjoyment through a deeper understanding of what the poem means to me and to others who have read it. Many teachers find that discussing poems with children can be one of the most rewarding of teaching experiences. With young children we may just be beginning the process of inviting them into the club of critical readers. To get them to listen to the poem, share their ideas and listen to what others have to say is quite an achievement in itself. Sometimes a poem will spark off more interesting discussion with one group of children than with another group. At times the 'spirit' of a poem may not seem to move children. As one child explained, in a matter-of-fact way: 'Some days we are good at talking about poems and some days we're not.'

One potential drawback to the conventional Literacy Hour is that there is not long for shared reading and discussion of a poem and for all the points and issues to be discussed. The trouble with teaching at pace, for a limited amount of time, is that it suits hare brains but not tortoise minds. A creative teacher will not feel constrained by the clock, and will use her professional judgement in orchestrating classroom discussion and reading time. We know that the oral groundwork of discussion, if it can be sustained, will enhance understanding and the quality of children's reading and writing.

Discussion can take place through shared reading with the class, through group discussion or through discussion with individual children.

Organising group reading and discussion of a poem

1 Divide the class into groups of four or five who are able to work together.

2 A scribe is chosen or appointed (this may be an adult helper) to write out ideas discussed by the group.

3 Children are given a poem to read together, then silently by themselves (or they may hear it on a tape).

4 They pause to think about the poem (thinking time).

5 Each child is invited to say one thing, or ask one question about the poem, which the scribe writes down.

6 Children in the group discuss each comment/question which have been written down.

7 In the plenary session each group shares what they have written and discussed.

Topics for discussion with individual or groups of children include:
- finding words that rhyme
- comparing and contrasting two poems (which do they prefer and why?)
- categorising poems (do they know/can they find another poem like this one?)
- ways to memorise a poem
- finding sound patterns within a poem (alliteration)
- choosing favourite rhymes, poems or poets
- creating their own titles for poems.

Any poem can be discussed and analysed in terms of its form and its content. Here are some elements to discuss about any poem:

Form
words (what does this word mean?)
lines (what is your favourite line?)
verses (favourite verse?)
chorus (repeated words?)
images (pictures in the mind?)
metaphors (pictures in words?)
sounds (sounds of words?)

Content
story (what is the poem about?)
feelings (is it a happy or sad poem)
thoughts (what does it make you think of?)
title (what title would you give this poem?)

The poet Blake once said, 'What is most poetic is also most private.' What discussion seeks to do is to help children give voice to their private thoughts and feelings, and to benefit from what others, including the teacher, has to say. But discussing a poem is only one way of responding to it. There are other ways to express what we think and feel.

Expressing

'*I like dance poems.*' Kate, aged six

A child has many forms of intelligence through which to make a creative response to a poem. Dance, drama, art, craft, music, movement, choral speaking, composing and creative writing all provide ways to express or re-create aspects, or the 'spirit', of a poem. Children can express a poem in their own way through any expressive medium, for example illustrating it with their own actions, pictures, drawings, models or musical accompaniment. The expressive arts allow children to enter the poet's world, and re-express the poet's ideas and images.

The following are some ways of extending a child's experience of a poem through creative response.

Twenty creative ways to respond to a poem

1   Illustrate a poem by drawing, painting or making a three-dimensional model.

2   Tape record the group reading a poem, to share later.

3   Close their eyes during a reading to 'see' the poem in their mind's eye.

4   Express the poem through movement and mime.

5   Create a collage of words, quotations and/or pictures about a theme or poet.

6   Make a mask or masks linked to the theme or poem.

7   Write a letter to the poet, with any questions you have about the poem.

8   Visit a library to review, survey and choose poetry books.

9   Invite a guest to discuss and share their favourite poems and to share yours.

10   Learn a chosen poem by heart; discuss the best ways of learning poems.

11   Create and discuss your own title for a given untitled poem.

12   Predict the words missing in a copy of a poem which has some words deleted (cloze).

13   Reconstruct the line or verse order of a poem which has had lines or verses jumbled.

14   Put into poetic form a nursery rhyme that has been written as prose.

15   Create music or sound effects to accompany a spoken poem.

16   Listen to taped readings of a poem.

17   Some 'wrong' words have been put in a poem. Decide which and propose alternatives.

18   Hunt special words or letters in a poem, underlining them in different colours.

19   Ask children to choose 'my favourite line' from a poem, to share, display and discuss.

20   Invite a poet to share, discuss and be questioned about their poetry.

Composing

Who alive can say,
'Thou art not a poet – mayest not tell thy dreams?'

John Keats

What inspires a poet to write poetry? Many poets would say that it is not nature, or the need to express their own feelings that most inspires them, but reading poetry. One of the problems for young children brought up solely on a diet of rhymes is that when it comes to writing poetry this narrow experience can limit their expressive capability. It is little wonder that many children say they 'can't' write poetry, when they have to concentrate on making rhymes, and abandon the effort to make meaning. This is a pity, since poetry is an ideal medium for young emergent writers.

In writing poetry children need not be bound by the narrow rules which govern nursery rhymes, and are free from the grammatical constraints of prose. They need not write whole sentences with finite verbs, or use capital letters and full stops, all of which emergent writers find difficult to remember even when they know the rules. In poetry meaning can be expressed in the fewest words, provided they are the 'important' words – nouns, adjectives, verbs and adverbs, not the repetitive connecting words, participles and the like which correct prose demands. For a young writer for whom forming every letter is an effort, poetry writing can provide an important freedom.

The easiest way to begin getting young children to write poetry is through shared writing, where the teacher takes the children's words and ideas and shapes them into a shared piece of writing. There is great value in adults modelling the writing process with children, by going through the composing process aloud in front of them, which could mean drafting out their own ideas or scribing the ideas of the children. 'Scribing' includes not only writing children's ideas for them but discussing their choice of words and phrases, helping them to cut out unnecessary words, and creating poetic effects (for example through repetition of words or lines) and so on. Shared or guided writing gives beginning writers the support they need. What they do as an individual or group supported by the guiding help of a teacher they will later be able to do on their own.

One teacher reports an example of this process in action with her class of 5-6 year olds:

Autumn leaves: first poems with five year olds

'We had read and discussed a poem about autumn leaves (see p 12). We collected our own autumn leaves, and as the children described the leaves they had brought in I wrote their words and phrases on the board. At first their descriptions were fairly simple; red, yellow, round, pointed and so on. I pressed them to say what they were *like* and to make comparisons, and I got expressions like 'thin as tissue paper', 'yellow as the sun' and 'crunchy as Rice Krispies'. I made a point of emphasising that this was their poem, using their words and ideas.

They went on to write a poem in pairs about their chosen leaf, with me focusing my help on one writer's group. We shared and displayed the children's writing in class, together with drawings of their leaves, and read the 'class' and 'individual' poems in assembly that week. None of the poems was brilliant, but the children had begun to see themselves as writers (or 'real poets' as I called them). They had learned about the process of writing, through jotting ideas, drafting, choosing best words, editing, proofreading and sharing with an audience. It was exciting to see five year olds acting as real writers, and to see the pride they took in their finished poems.'

Here is one of the poems:

Autumn Leaf

My autumn leaf

is red and brown

it has tiny specks

all over it

like a banana

it has a pointed end

like a star.

Anna, aged five

Reading, responding to and writing poems can enable children to voice thoughts and feelings that might otherwise remain trapped, inarticulate and unspoken. Poetry can empower children by offering them many voices, many messages, many tongues.

Giving children the voice to express and share their experience can be one of the most rewarding aspects in teaching literacy. The following is an example of a five year old sharing thoughts about his special pet. First he wrote it as prose, then was shown how to write it in lines as poetry by choosing his best words and putting them in the best order:

I have a pet koala

he is all fluffy and grey

and he is missing an eye

when mummy put him

in the washing machine

he has only one black eye

it is a pity

he's stuffed

Tom, aged five

Ted Hughes described the act of writing poetry as 'all out flowing exertion for a short concentrated period, in a particular direction.' What the teacher does is to provide the direction, introduce children to interesting poems, and support them in drafting their own poems. Once created they can be communicated through publication, to provide purpose and an audience, first in the writing group or class, then beyond the class in the school, local library or public space, or to a range of possible audiences, such as other children and other schools, on the internet.

Poetry may do many things, help children to see, to hear and to feel, to understand themselves and others better, to help them grow as people and to develop their understanding of words as tools for thinking. It is something that can enrich them for the rest of their lives. As Jamie said of his favourite poem: 'I can show it to others, but it will always be mine.'

Further reading

Brownjohn S (1994), *Poetry Express (series)*, Aylesbury: Ginn

Carter D (1998), *Teaching Poetry in the Primary School*, London: David Fulton Publishers

Fisher, R (1995), *Teaching Children to Think*, Cheltenham: Stanley Thornes

Fisher R (1995) *Teaching Children to Learn*, Cheltenham: Stanley Thornes

Fisher R (1998) *Teaching Thinking: Philosophical Enquiry in the Classroom*, London: Cassell

Fisher R (1999), *Head Start : How to Develop Your Child's Mind*, London: Souvenir Press

The 'Stories for Thinking' series

Fisher R (1999) *First Stories for Thinking*, Oxford: Nash Pollock

Fisher R (1996), *Stories for Thinking*, Oxford: Nash Pollock

Fisher R (1997), *Poems for Thinking*, Oxford: Nash Pollock

Fisher R (1997), *Games for Thinking*, Oxford: Nash Pollock

Merrick B and Balaam J (1990), *Exploring Poetry 5-8*, Sheffield: NATE Publications

Powling C and Styles M (Eds) (1997), *A Guide to Poetry 0-13*, London: Centre for Language in Primary Education

Wilson A (Ed) (1998), *The Poetry Book for Primary Schools*, London: Poetry Society

SAPERE (Society for the Advancement of Philosophical Enquiry and Reflection in Education), the national organisation for philosophy with children
Website: www.sapere.net

ROBERT FISHER
Dr Robert Fisher, Brunel University,
300 St. Margarets Road, Twickenham TW1 1PT
Website: www.teachingthinking.net

Poems

1

Autumn Leaves

See autumn leaves
float down
brown as chocolate
purple as a plum
5   yellow as the sun
red as strawberry
speckled as eggs
spotted white with snow
ends point like a star
10   or curl like a dog's ear
thin as a feather

smell autumn leaves
where they fall
like flakes of fire
15   burnt brown and red

feel autumn leaves
smooth as silk
crisp and stiff
rough to touch

20   hear autumn leaves
under foot they crunch
like cornflakes
and crumble to pieces

autumn leaves
25   whisper
as they fall

Robert Fisher

Thinking about the poem

Key question: What does the poem mean?

1   What time of year is autumn?

2   Why do some leaves fall off trees in autumn?

3   What colours does the poem say autumn leaves are?

4   What does 'speckled' mean (line 7)? What else is speckled?

5   What are the ends of autumn leaves like (lines 9-11)?

6   Why are some autumn leaves described as 'burnt' (line 15)?

7   What does the poem say autumn leaves feel like to touch? Do you agree?

8   When does the poem say you can hear autumn leaves?

9   What does it mean 'autumn leaves whisper as they fall' (last verse)?

10   Which line in the poem do you like best? Are there lines you do not like? Why?

Thinking about the senses

Key question: What are your senses?

1   What are the five senses?

2   Why do we have senses?

3   Could we live without one of our senses?

4   Which do you think is most important: to see, hear, taste, touch or smell? Why?

5   If you had to lose one of them which would it be?

6   Which do you prefer, to listen to a story or read it in a book? Why?

7   Which do you prefer, to see your food, smell it or taste it? Why?

8   What do you most like to touch? Describe how it feels to touch.

9   What do you most like to smell? Can you describe the smell?

10   What have you seen, heard, tasted, touched and smelled today?

Further activities

• Discuss how to read the poem, with pauses, to help it make sense.

• Ask children for new similes for lines from the poem eg 'brown as - (as in 'brown as a berry/ a bird/ mud) ', 'purple as -' , 'yellow as -'.

• Choose a topic to describe something using the senses eg 'See - (as in 'See through the window'), hear -, smell -, taste -, feel -'.

• Collect, study and draw or paint autumn leaves. Describe and display your leaves.

• Have a sense quiz eg identify things by taste, touch or smell while blindfolded.

2

The Colours

The colours live
Between black and white
In a land that we
Know best by sight
5   But knowing best
Isn't everything
For colours dance
And colours sing,
And colours laugh
10   And colours cry -
Turn off the light
And colours die,
And they make you feel
Every feeling there is
15   From the grumpiest grump
To the fizziest fizz.
And you and you and I
Know well
Each has a taste
20   And each has a smell
And each has a wonderful
Story to tell -

Mary O'Neill

Thinking about the poem

Key question: What does the poem mean?

1   What do the first lines mean when they say 'The colours live between black and white'?
2   What do we know 'best by sight'?
3   What do you think the poet means by 'Knowing best/Isn't everything'?
4   In what way do colours 'dance'?
5   In what ways do colours 'sing'?
6   What does the poem mean when it says ' colours laugh/And colours cry'(lines 9-10)?
7   When do colours 'die'? Why do they 'die'?
8   What kind of feelings do colours make you feel?
9   Do colours have a taste or smell?
10 What kind of story could a colour tell?

Thinking about colours

Key question: What are colours?

1   Which is your favourite colour? Why?
2   Does everything have a colour?
3   How many colours do you know/can you name?
4   How many colours can you see?
5   Could there be a colour that you have never seen? Why?
6   Could there be a colour that no-one has ever seen? Why?
7   Can you say which is the most important colour? Why?
8   What would happen in the world if everything was the same colour?
9   What would happen if things kept changing colour?
10 If you were a different colour would that make you a different person?

Further activities

• Write 'colour' and ask children to write or say as many colour words as they can.
• Choose a colour and ask children to complete sentences describing it eg 'Red is ...'
• Write a poem or story about the colours you like best.
• Make a colour display of articles of one colour eg stones, paper, cloth, flowers etc.
• Make charts or circles showing colours from hot to cold, or shades from black to white.

3

Daddy Fell into the Pond

Everyone grumbled. The sky was gray.
We had nothing to do and nothing to say.
We were nearing the end of a dismal day,
And there seemed to be nothing beyond,
5   *Then*
       Daddy fell into the pond !

And everyone's face grew merry and bright,
And Timothy danced for sheer delight.
'Give me the camera, quick, oh quick!
10   He's crawling out of the duckweed.' *Click*!
Then the gardener suddenly slapped his knee,
And doubled up, shaking silently,
And the ducks all quacked as if they were daft
And it sounded as if the old drake laughed.

15   Oh, there wasn't a thing that didn't respond
    When
       Daddy fell into the pond!

                     Alfred Noyes

Thinking about the poem

Key question: What does the poem mean?

1   The first line says 'Everyone grumbled.' Why do you think they were they grumbling?

2   What was the weather like?

3   What time of day was it?

4   What do you think Daddy was doing before he fell into the pond?

5   How do you think he could have fallen into the pond?

6   Why did everyone's face turn merry and bright?

7   What did Timothy do? Why did he do this?

8   What did the gardener do? Why did he do it?

9   What did the ducks and old drake do? Why?

10   What do you think happened next?

Thinking about accidents

Key question: What is an accident?

1   What is an accident?

2   Has an accident ever happened to you? Describe what happened.

3   Why did it happen? Why do accidents happen?

4   Have you ever seen an accident happen to someone else? Describe what happened.

5   What might have caused the accident?

6   Do accidents happen to everybody? Why?

7   Where do accidents happen? Who helps when an accident happens?

8   Can anything be done to stop accidents?

9   What should you do if you accidentally hurt someone?

10   What does it mean to do something 'accidentally'?

Further activities

- Cover every verb in the text. Ask the children to think what each missing verb could be.
- Find the words printed in italics. Discuss why they are written in italics.
- Tell or write a story about someone who fell into a pond.
- Find out about local emergency services – police, fire brigade and ambulance service.
- Make a list of possible accidents, and discuss what to do if an accident happens.

4

Emma Hackett's Newsbook

Last night my mum
Got really mad
And threw a jam tart
At my dad.
5 Dad lost his temper
Then with mother,
Threw one at her
And hit my brother.
My brother thought
10 It was my sister,
Threw two at her
But somehow missed her.
My sister,
She is only three,
15 Hurled four at him
And one at me!
I said I wouldn't
Stand for that.
Aimed one at her
20 And hit the cat.
The cat jumped up
Like he'd been shot,
And landed
In the baby's cot.
25 The baby -
Quietly sucking his thumb -
Then started howling
For my mum.
At which mum
30 Got *really* mad,
And threw a Swiss roll
At my dad.

Allan Ahlberg

Thinking about the poem

Key question: What does the poem mean?
1   When did mum get really mad?
2   What does 'getting really mad' mean?
3   What might have made her get really mad?
4   What did she do when she got really mad?
5   What happened when Dad lost his temper?
6   What did the other people do? Why did they do this?
7   What made mum really mad? Why was this?
8   How do you think it all ended?
9   Why is this poem called 'Emma Hackett's Newsbook'?
10   Do you think what the poem says really happened? Why?

Thinking about quarrelling

Key question: Why do people quarrel?
1   How many people does it need to have a quarrel?
2   Have you ever been in a quarrel? Describe the quarrel.
3   Why did you quarrel? Why do people quarrel?
4   Have you ever seen or heard people quarrelling? Give an example.
5   What might have caused the quarrel?
6   Have you ever quarrelled with a friend? Why (or why not)?
7   Have you ever tried to stop a quarrel? What happened? Why?
8   Is it ever a good thing to quarrel? Why, or why not?
9   Why do people in families who love each other sometimes quarrel?
10   What makes you lose your temper?

Further activities

*   Cover all the words at the end of each line. Can children predict what the end-words could be?
*   Identify the punctuation in the poem and discuss its use eg What is a full stop for?
*   Ask children if they can reconstruct all the events in the poem in the right order.
*   Discuss what each character might be thinking at different stages of the story.
*   Act out a story about a quarrel between two people that was stopped by a third.

5

Fairy Story

I went into the wood one day
And there I walked and lost my way

When it was so dark I could not see
A little creature came to me

5   He said if I would sing a song
The time would not be very long

But first I must let him hold my hand tight
Or else the wood would give me a fright

I sang a song, he let me go
10   But now I am home again there is nobody I know.

Stevie Smith

Thinking about the poem

Key question: What does the poem mean?

1   Why do you think the person in the poem went into the woods?
2   What does it mean 'there I walked and lost my way?' How do you lose your way?
3   Why was it 'so dark' I could not see?
4   What do you think the 'little creature' could have been like?
5   Why did he want the person in the poem to sing a song?
6   Why did he want to 'hold my hand very tight'?
7   What kind of song do you think the person sang to the little creature?
8   Why did the creature let the person go?
9   What does the last line mean: 'But now I am home again there is nobody I know'?
10   Why do you think this poem is called 'Fairy Story'?

Thinking about stories

Key question: What is a story?

1   What kind of story is a 'fairy story'?
2   What kind of characters are in fairy stories?
3   What kind of things happen in fairy stories?
4   Where do fairy stories happen? What kind of places (settings) are in fairy stories?
5   Can you remember a fairy story? What happened in the story?
6   Could a fairy story be true? Could it really happen? Explain why.
7   Could a fairy story be written as a poem?
8   Could a fairy story be told without words? Could it be told in pictures?
9   What is the difference between a fairy story and real life?
10   Could someone's life be like a fairy story? Explain how or why, or why not.

Further activities

- Ask children to retell the story of the poem as if it had happened to them.
- Make a deliberate error in reading a word. Can children spot which word was wrong?
- Ask children to begin a story 'I went into the wood one day ...' and continue it.
- Collect fairy story books. Show two versions of a story. Which do they prefer? Why?
- Invite children to act out their own version of a fairy story.

6
Five Little Chickens

Said the first little chicken,
With a queer little squirm,
'Oh. I wish I could find
A fat little worm!'

5   Said the next little chicken,
With an odd little shrug,
'Oh, I wish I could find
A fat little bug!'

Said the third little chicken,
10 With a sharp little squeal,
'Oh, I wish I could find
Some nice yellow meal!'

Said the fourth little chicken,
With a small sigh of grief,
15 'Oh, I wish I could find
A green little leaf.'

Said the fifth little chicken,
With a faint little moan,
'Oh, I wish I could find
20 A wee gravel-stone!'

Now, see here,' said the mother,
From the green garden-patch,
'If you want any breakfast,
You must come and scratch.'

Anon

Thinking about the poem

Key question: What does the poem mean?

1   What did the first little chicken wish? Why?

2   The first chicken gave 'a queer little squirm'. What is that?

3   What did the second little chicken wish?

4   Why did the chicken give 'an odd little shrug'?

5   What did the third little chicken wish?

6   What was the third little chicken's voice like?

7   What did the fourth and fifth chicken wish? How did they say it?

8   What is 'a wee gravel-stone'? Why did the fifth chicken wish to find one?

9   Why did the mother say 'If you want any breakfast/You must come and scratch'?

10 Who do you think wrote this poem? Why was it written?

Thinking about wishes

Key question: What do people wish for?

1   What is a wish?

2   Have you ever wished for something to happen?

3   Has one of your wishes ever come true? Describe what happened.

4   Some people hope for things. Is wishing the same as hoping?

5   Some people pray for things. Is wishing the same as praying?

6   Is there any magic that will help a wish come true? Why?

7   Does wishing for something help it to come true? Why?

8   Is there any point in wishing for things?

9   Do we all wish for different things? Why?

10 Are there some things we all wish for? If so, what are they?

Further activities

• Discuss and choose an alternative title for the poem.

• Find the words the chickens say and write them in speech bubbles linked to a picture of each chicken.

• Think and write down as many words as you can that are about chickens.

• Write a poem using this poem as a model, adding your own words ie 'Said the first little -, With a - - -, 'Oh I wish I could find, A -'

• Who is Anon? Ask children to find poems by Anon. Which is their favourite Anon poem?

7

I Saw a Peacock

I saw a peacock with a fiery tail,
I saw a blazing comet drop down hail,
I saw a cloud with ivy circled round,
I saw a sturdy oak creep on the ground,
5   I saw a little ant swallow a whale,
I saw a raging sea brim full of ale,
I saw a drinking glass sixteen foot deep,
I saw a well full of men's tears that weep,
I saw their eyes all in a flame of fire,
10   I saw a house as big as the moon or higher,
I saw the sun in the middle of the night,
I saw the man that saw this wondrous sight.

Anon

Thinking about the poem

Key question: What does the poem mean?

1   What is strange about a peacock with a fiery tail?

2   Could a 'blazing comet drop down hail'? Why?

3   What does ivy circle round?

4   What creeps on the ground?

5   What could swallow a whale?

6   What is the strangest line (or sight) in this poem?

7   Did the poet see all these things? How do we know?

8   Could this poem be true? Why do you think so?

9   Do you think the poem was written recently or a long time ago? Why?

10   What title would you give this poem?

Thinking about true and not true

Key question: How can you tell if something is true or not true?

1   Do you believe everything people tell you? Why, or why not?

2   Do you believe everything you read? Why or why not?

3   Has anyone ever told you something that was not true? Explain what happened.

4   Has anyone told you something that was true, but you did not believe them? Explain.

5   Do some people exaggerate? What does 'exaggerate' mean?

6   Can something be true even though you have never seen it? Give an example.

7   Do some people pretend to see things they have never seen?

8   Are there some people you would always believe? Who? Why?

9   What is the strangest sight you have ever seen?

10   What us the strangest thing you have ever heard? Was it true? How do you know?

Further activities

- Discuss how the poem was written, and what is strange or marvellous about each thing eg 'peacock', 'comet' etc.

- Discuss what a rhyme is. Identify rhyming words, and discuss possible alternative rhymes.

- Focus on consonant clusters eg bl-, cl-, st-, gr-, sw-, br-, fl- (initial) -ck, -ng, -tle, -nt, -ll, -ss, -dle (end). List other words with these blends.

- Discuss and write about 'The most fantastic thing I've seen' (link these to make a poem).

- Choose one item in the poem to paint in as colourful and fantastic way as possible.

8

I'd rather be

I'd rather be hot than cold
I'd rather be young than old
I'd rather be alive than dead
I'd rather be here than in bed
5   I'd rather be a bat than a ball
I'd rather be too short than too tall
I'd rather be thick than thin
I'd rather play out than in
I'd rather be a knife than a fork
10   I'd rather eat beef than eat pork
I'd rather be a dog than a cat
I'd rather be a shoe than a hat
I'd rather be a peach than a pear
I'd rather be a bird than a bear
15   I'd rather be the day than the night
I'd rather be friends than fight
I'd rather be me than be you
but I'd rather not choose what to do!

Robert Fisher

Thinking about the poem

Key question: What does the poem mean?

1   Why do you think the poet would rather be hot than cold?

2   Why do you think the poet would rather be young than old?

3   Why do you think the poet would rather be too short than too tall?

4   Why do you think the poet would rather play out than in?

5   Why do you think the poet would rather be a dog than a cat?

6   Why do you think the poet would rather be a shoe than a hat?

7   Why do you think the poet would rather be a bird than a bear?

8   Why do you think the poet would rather be the day than the night?

9   Why do you think the poet would rather be me than you?

10   Why do you think the poet would rather not choose what to do?

Thinking about choices

Key question: What choices have you got?

1   Would you rather choose or be told what to do? Why?

2   What do your mum and dad allow you to choose?

3   What are you allowed to choose in school?

4   What do you choose to do at playtime?

5   What would you choose to do that you are not allowed to do?

6   Is it sometimes difficult to choose? When? Give an example.

7   Who helps you choose things?

8   Do we choose our friends?

9   If you could choose everything about your best friend, what would they be like?

10   If you were asked to choose the best thing about you what would it be?

Further activities

- Ask children to make up their own lines beginning 'I'd rather be … than …'

- Discuss words that are opposites eg 'hot and -', 'young and -', 'alive and -' etc.

- Cover up rhyming words at ends of lines. Can children suggest what words might rhyme?

- Give children two of the same thing eg toys, pictures, books. Ask them to choose their favourite one and say why.

- Draw portraits and choose one aspect of the person to write about eg 'The best thing about – is …'

9

In the Dark Dark Wood

In the dark, dark wood,
There was a dark, dark house,
And in that dark, dark house,
There was a dark, dark room,
5   And in that dark, dark room,
There was a dark, dark cupboard,
And in that dark, dark cupboard,
There was a dark, dark shelf,
And on that dark, dark shelf,
10   There was a dark, dark box,
And in that dark, dark box,
There was a GHOST!

Anon

Yesterday Upon the Stair

Yesterday upon the stair,
I met a man who wasn't there;
He wasn't there again today,
I wish, I wish he'd go away.

Anon

Thinking about the poems

Key question: What do the poems mean?

1 Is there a difference between a 'dark wood' and a 'dark, dark wood'? If so, what?

2 What does 'dark' mean? Why is the wood dark?

3 Are there different kinds of dark? Is the dark of a dark wood the same as a dark house?

4 What might be dark about a house? Are there other words for 'dark'?

5 What was in the dark house/ in the dark room/in the dark cupboard?

6 What do you think the box might have looked like? What was in the box?

7 What might the ghost be like?

8 In then second poem could the poet really see a man who isn't there?

9 Why does the poet want the man who isn't there to go away?

10 What do you like or not like about these poems? Which do you like better? Why?

Thinking about ghosts

Key question: Do ghosts exist?

1 What is a ghost story? What is a ghost?

2 Have you ever seen a ghost? If so, what happened?

3 Have you seen something that looked like a ghost but was not a ghost?

4 Is it possible to see things that do not really exist? Explain why.

5 Do you know a story or poem about a ghost? If so, which story or poem?

6 Have you ever seen a film about a ghost? If so, what do you remember about the film?

7 Have you ever written or told a ghost story?

8 Do strange noises at night frighten you? Why, or why not?

9 Some people have pretend friends they talk to. Is a pretend friend a ghost?

10 Do you believe that ghosts exist? Why or why not?

Further activities

- Cover the poem and ask children to recall the words of the poem in sequence.

- Use the poem as a model for children to add words eg 'In the dark, dark ... there was a ...'

- Brainstorm words connected with 'ghosts'.

- Find , display and discuss books, stories and poems about ghosts eg *Ghosts Galore*, a poetry anthology edited by Robert Fisher (Faber).

- Create a book of the poem, with a drawing to illustrate each line.

10
Lone Dog

I'm a lean dog, a keen dog, a wild dog and lone,
I'm a rough dog, a tough dog, hunting on my own!
I'm a bad dog, a mad dog, teasing silly sheep;
I love to sit and bay the moon and keep fat souls from sleep.

5 I'll never be a lap dog, licking dirty feet,
A sleek dog, a meek dog, cringing for my meat.
Not for me the fireside, the well-filled plate,
But shut door and sharp stone and cuff and kick and hate.

Not for me the other dogs, running by my side,
10 Some have run a short while, but none of them would bide.
O mine is still the lone trail, the hard trail, the best,
Wide wind and wild stars and the hunger of the quest.

Irene McLeod

Thinking about the poem

Key question: What does the poem mean?

1 Who is speaking in the poem?

2 What does the poem say the lone dog is like?

3 How does the dog keep 'fat souls from sleep'?

4 What kind of dog does the lone dog not want to be?

5 Why for the lone dog is there a 'shut door and sharp stone and cuff and kick and hate' (line 8)?

6 Why are there no other dogs running with the lone dog?

7 Why does the dog think 'the lone trail, the hard trail' is the best?

8 What do you think 'the hunger of the quest' means (last line)?

9 Do you think the lone dog is male or female? Why?

10 Would you like to be the lone dog? Why?

Thinking about being alone

Key question: What is it like being alone?

1 When are you alone?

2 When is it good to be alone?

3 When is it not good to be alone?

4 Can you be alone when there is someone else there?

5 When you are alone are you lonely?

6 Is being alone the same as being lonely?

7 Which animals live alone, and which live with others?

8 Do you prefer to be alone or with others? Why?

9 If you felt lonely, what could you do about it?

10 How would you help someone who was feeling lonely?

Further activities

• Write down and discuss the questions which the children would like to ask the lone dog.

• Collect and list adjectives ('describing words') children could use to describe a dog.

• Look for rhyming words in each line of the poem. How many can the children find?

• Write or tell a story, in the first person, imagining that you are a lone dog.

• Draw or paint a picture to illustrate the life of the lone dog.

11

My New Year's Resolutions

I will not throw the cat out the window
Or put a frog in my sister's bed
I will not tie my brother's shoelaces together
Nor jump from the roof of dad's shed.
5   I shall remember my aunt's next birthday
And tidy my room once a week
I'll not moan at mum's cooking (Ugh! fish fingers again!)
Nor give her any more of my cheek.
I will not pick my nose if I can help it
10   I shall hang up my clothes, comb my hair,
I will say 'Please' and 'Thank you' (even when I don't mean it)
And never spit or shout or even swear.
I shall write each day in my diary
Try my hardest to be helpful at school
15   I shall help old ladies cross the roads (even if they don't want to)
And when others are rude I'll stay cool.
I'll go to bed with the owls, be up with the larks
And close every door behind me
I shall squeeze from the bottom every toothpaste tube
20   And stay where trouble can't find me.
I shall start again, turn over a new leaf,
leave my bad old ways forever
Shall I start them this year, or next year
Shall I sometime, or ..... ?

Robert Fisher

Thinking about the poem

Key question: What does the poem mean?

1   Why does the poet say 'I will not throw the cat out the window'?
2   What will the poet say he will not do to his sister and brother?
3   Why do you think he says he will not jump from the roof of his dad's shed?
4   What will he do for his aunt and his mum?
5   Why does he want to say 'please' and 'thank you' even when he doesn't mean it (line 11)?
6   What is he going to try to do each day (line 13)? Why ?
7   What does it mean 'to turn over a new leaf' (line 21)?
8   What do you think is the worst of his bad old ways?
9   When will he start to leave his bad old ways?
10   Do you think he will do as he says?

Thinking about me

Key question: What kind of person am I?

1   Can you think of one good thing about yourself?
2   Is everything about you good? Are you perfect? Is anyone perfect?
3   Can you think of one bad thing about yourself or bad habit you have got?
4   Is there something about you that you could change to make better? Explain.
5   Is there something about you that you cannot change? Explain.
6   Do you find it easy or hard to be good? Give an example.
7   Is it easy or hard to be bad? Give an example.
8   Do you ever talk to yourself? When? What do you say?
9   Does it help to talk to yourself? Why?
10   What kind of person are you? How would you describe yourself?

Further activities

- Ask children to recall details of the story in sequence, adding actions in mime.
- Cover all the verbs in the poems and ask children what the missing words might be.
- Discuss the idea of 'New Year's Resolutions'. Ask children to make up their own.
- Draw a picture showing one bad habit, and its opposite. Explain your drawing.
- Make a chart illustrating 'This year', 'Next year', 'Sometime' and 'Never'.

12
Nonsense

I went to school tomorrow,
And took a front seat at the back.
I walked through a door that was closed,
And broke a front bone in my back.
5   The teacher she gave me some chocolate,
I ate it and gave it her back.
I caught a bus home and walked it,
And that's why I never came back!

Anon

The Man in the Wilderness

The Man in the Wilderness asked of me,
How many strawberries grow in the sea?'
I answered him as I thought good,
'As many red herrings as grow in the wood.'

5   The Man in the Wilderness asked me why
His hen could swim, and his pig could fly.
I answered him briskly as I thought best,
'Because they were born in a cuckoo's nest.'

The Man in the Wilderness asked me to tell
10   The sands in the sea and I counted them well.
Says he with a grin, 'And not one more?'
I answered him bravely, 'You go and make sure!'

Anon

Thinking about the poems

Key question: What do the poems mean?

1 Does 'I went to school tomorrow' make sense? Why?
2 Can you take a front seat at the back? Why?
3 Could someone walk through a door that was closed? Why?
4 Could you have a front bone in your back? Why?
5 Could you eat chocolate and give it back? Why?
6 Why does the first poem end 'And that's why I never came back!'?
7 Who do you think 'The Man in the Wilderness' might be?
8 Which is the strangest question that the 'The Man' asked? Why is it strange?
9 What do you think the best answer to the Man's questions was? Why?
10 What do you like or not like about these poems?

Thinking about nonsense

Key question: What is nonsense?

1 What does 'nonsense' mean?
2 What is a nonsense poem? Do you know any nonsense poems?
3 Can one word be nonsense? Why?
4 Do you know, or can you make up, a word that is nonsense?
5 Does every word have a meaning?
6 How do we know what words mean?
7 Do some words have more than one meaning? Can you think of an example?
8 Does every sentence make sense? Can you think of a sentence that makes no sense?
9 Just because you do not understand something, does that mean it is nonsense?
10 If you do not understand something, what should you do?

Further activities

- Cover up words at the end of each line. Ask children to suggest how each line might end.
- Play 'Hunt the vowel (or letter)'. Show a letter and see how many of them children can find it in the poem.
- Ask children to make up sentences or questions that are nonsense.
- Find and read nonsense poems or rhymes eg by Edward Lear, Lewis Carroll, Spike Milligan.
- Illustrate a favourite nonsense rhyme, and create your own Book of Nonsense.

13
Public Speaking

When cows enquire 'How do you do?'
They moo.

When horses give you the time of day,
They neigh.

5 When dogs pass the odd remark,
They bark.

When ducks need to answer back,
They quack.

When cats wholeheartedly concur,
10 They purr

When pigs are moved to file a report,
They snort.

When owls are asked to make a speech,
They screech.

15 When sheep are forced to think on their feet,
They bleat.

But when I'm called upon to speak,
I squeak.

I mumble and mutter,
20 I stumble and stutter,
And tie my tongue into a knot.

What have they got
That I have not?

Sandra Willingham

Thinking about the poem

Key question: What does the poem mean?

1 What does the first line mean; 'enquire 'How do you do?' Could a cow's moo mean this?

2 What do the words 'give you the time of day' mean (line 3)? Could a horse's neigh mean this?

3 What sort of 'odd remark' might a dog wish to make (line 5)?

4 When might ducks want to answer back? What might a quack mean?

5 What does 'When cats wholeheartedly concur' mean (line 9)?

6 What does 'to file a report' mean (line 11)? What might pigs want to say in a report?

7 What sort of speech might owls want to make?

8 When might sheep be forced to think on their feet?

9 What happens to the poet when she is asked to speak?

10 How would you answer the last question? What have animals got that the poet has not?

Thinking about speaking

Key question: What is speaking?

1 Do you like speaking to other people? Why or why not?

2 Who do you like speaking to? Why?

3 Who do you not like speaking to? Why?

4 Is it sometimes difficult to say things? Why, or why not?

5 Why do some people find saying things difficult to do? How could you help them?

6 Have you ever been 'tongue-tied' and not been able to speak? What happened?

7 Are you good at listening to other people? When do you not listen? Why?

8 Do people always listen to you? What do you/would you feel like if they did not listen?

9 Do you think animals speak to each other (or to people)? Can you say why?

10 Which do you think is more important speaking or listening? Why?

Further activities

• Ask children to read the poem out loud, adding appropriate sound effects (animal noises).

• Show animal pictures and discuss words for the sounds they make.

• Brainstorm and list as many different words that could be used instead of 'said'.

• Paint/draw animals, adding words for what they might be thinking or trying to say.

• Hold a public speaking competition where children read/recite a favourite poem to others.

14
Secret Things

Sometimes people say
they know something I don't know.
I ask what it is
and say, 'Tell me.'
5   They say, 'You won't get the secret from me.'

Sometimes I ask a question
and they won't answer.
I say, 'Why not?'
and they say
10 'You will understand some day.'

Sometimes I think things
I cannot say,
they are secret things
I don't talk to anyone about –
15 a worry, fear, hope or doubt.

Sometimes they say
'What are you thinking?'
I tell them what they want to know,
but they would not understand all the things
20 I think and do not say — secret things!

Robert Fisher

Thinking about the poem

Key question: What does the poem mean?

1   Who might the people be in line 1 who say they know something I don't know?

2   Why do you think they say 'You won't get the secret from me' (line 5)?

3   What question might the poet be asking that 'they won't answer' (line 7)?

4   What do you think they mean by saying: 'You will understand some day' (line10)?

5   What does the poet mean: 'I think things I cannot say' (lines 11-12)?

6   The poem says a secret thing could be a worry. What is a worry? Give an example.

7   The poem says a secret thing could be a fear, hope or doubt. What could they be?

8   The poem says a secret thing could be a hope. What is a hope? Give an example.

9   The poem says a secret thing could be a doubt. What is a doubt? Give an example.

10   Why does the poet think other people 'would not understand all the things I think and do not say' (lines 19-20)?

Thinking about secrets

Key question: What are secret things?

1   What is a secret? Give an example of a secret.

2   Do your friends ever tell you secrets?

3   Do your friends know secrets they don't tell you? How do you know?

4   Do you tell secrets to your friends? What kind of secrets?

5   Do you think secret things that you never talk about?

6   Does everybody think secret things? (Does your teacher think secret things?)

7   Why don't we always know what other people are thinking?

8   Do you have a secret hiding place, secret plans, a secret friend?

9   When someone tells a secret is it always the truth? Why or why not?

10   Is it a good thing to keep secrets?

Further activities

- Find the speech marks in the poem and re-read it with children saying the spoken parts.

- Ask children to complete the sentences: 'Sometimes people say ...', 'Sometimes I ask a question ...', and 'Sometimes I think ...'

- Create a box containing written worries, fears, hopes or doubts contributed by children.

- Read and discuss 'The Secret Brother' by Elizabeth Jennings (in *Ghosts Galore* ed R. Fisher, Faber, p 18).

- Play Chinese Whispers (see *Games for Thinking* in this series, p 47), to investigate secret messages.

15
Sleeping Beauty

When she was a baby
but one month old,
fairies came with gifts,
not of flowers or gold,
5　but promises of beauty,
of happiness and health.

In stormed a bad fairy
not invited to the party,
with her evil promise,
10　that one unlucky day
the princess would prick
her finger, and would die.

Only one fairy left,
what hope could she give?
15　What good is joy
if you cannot live?
We cannot stop bad luck,
but we can make it better.'

So for a hundred years
20　the princess slept,
and sometimes she dreamt
of a daring prince who would,
with a sword and a kiss,
25　turn bad luck into good.

Robert Fisher

Thinking about the poem

Key question: What does the poem mean?

1 The poem talks about a baby. What is a baby? How old was the baby?

2 Who was invited to the party? What gifts did they bring?

3 What is a 'good fairy'?

4 Who was not invited to the party? Why?

5 Why did the the bad fairy make an evil promise? What was it? Why was it evil?

6 What does it mean, 'What good is joy if you cannot live?' (lines 16-17)?

7 What could the good fairy do to make the bad luck better?

8 How long did the princess sleep? Is that possible?

9 What did she dream of ? Why did she dream this?

10 What does the poem not tell you about the story?

Thinking about luck

Key question: What is luck?

1 What does it mean to be lucky?

2 What does it mean to be unlucky?

3 Can you give an example of something that is lucky?

4 Can you give an example of something that is unlucky?

5 Have you ever had good luck, or bad luck ?

6 Why do people want babies to have good luck?

7 Some people have things they think bring them luck. What is a lucky charm?

8 Do you think that things like charms can bring good luck or bad luck?

9 Are there any times when you wish for good luck?

10 Can people be lucky all the time? Why?

Further activities

• Look for two words in the poem that rhyme. Find other words to rhyme with these.

• Write the sentence 'When I was a baby ..' and ask children to finish it in different ways.

• Ask children to act out giving a baby a present of their choice and what they would say.

• Find, discuss and display a lucky bracelet or lucky charms.

• Discuss promises. Ask children to think of and write a promise to keep.

16
Some Times I Dream

Sometimes I lie upon my bed
And let my dreams float round my head.
Sometimes I think the strangest things
Like I'm a bird and I've got wings!

5   Sometimes I dream I'll fly away
To where the sun shines every day?
Sometimes I think I'd rather be
Any kind of person but me.

Sometimes I think I'll be a dog,
10   A cat or lion, monkey or frog!
Sometimes I dream I'll run away
Or that today is my birthday.

Sometimes I lie upon my bed
And let my dreams float round my head,
15   Happy that my thoughts are free
And happy just being me.

Robert Fisher

My Dream

I dreamed a dream next Tuesday week,
Beneath the apple trees, I thought my eyes were big pork pies,
And my nose was stilton cheese.
The clock struck twenty minutes to six,
5   When a frog sat on my knee;
I asked him to lend me eighteen pence,
But he borrowed a pound off me.

Anon

Thinking about the poem

Key question: What does the poem mean?

1   In the first two lines do you think the poet is awake or asleep? Why?

2   What might be one of the 'strangest things' the poet is thinking (line 3)?

3   What place might it be' where the sun shines every day' (line 6)?

4   Why might the poet want to be 'any kind of person but me' (line 8)?

5   Why would the poet want to be 'a dog, a cat or lion, monkey or frog' (line 10)?

6   Why might the poet want to dream of running away (line 11)?

7   Why does he sometimes dream 'that today is my birthday' (line 12)?

8   When he says 'sometimes I lie upon my bed', when and how often might this be?

9   Why does he feel 'happy that my thoughts are free'(line 15)?

10   Do you think the poet is 'happy just being me'? Why?

Thinking about dreams

Key question: What is a dream?

1   When do you have dreams?

2   Can you dream during the day? What is a daydream?

3   What is the difference between a daydream and dreaming while you are asleep?

4   Can you remember your dreams? Tell about one dream you have had.

5   Are there some dreams you cannot remember? Why is this?

6   Do impossible things happen in dreams? Give an example.

7   Can you make yourself dream something? Can you control your dreams?

8   Do you think dreams ever come true? Can you give an example?

9   Do you ever have frightening dreams (nightmares)? Tell about one.

10   Do people have the same dreams, or does everyone have different dreams? Why is this?

Further activities

* Ask children to recount all the different kinds of dream that are in the poem(s).

* Ask children to identify which words and lines are repeated in the poem.

* Read the poem making some deliberate mistakes. Can the children spot each mistake?

* Draw or paint a picture of a strange dream. (See the dream-like pictures of Marc Chagall.)

* Compile a Book of Dreams written or told by the children.

17
That Cat!

Scat cat!
Don't come back for more,
there's a poor dead sparrow
by the kitchen door.

5   Drat cat!
With your long sharp claw,
took blood from the bird
that's left on the floor.

Brat cat!
10   I'm not at all sure
I want you back,
your slaughter's a bore.

Fat cat!
Eating fish that's raw
15   from your dish each day,
you live by your law
and know no other way.

Fancy that cat!
I should not ignore
20   that your're not just a pet,
you're a hunter and more,
you're my one true friend.

So welcome back cat!
Come and lick your paw,
25   there's fish in a dish
and a place to snore,
you're the purr-fect cat for me.

Robert Fisher

Thinking about the poem

Key question: What does the poem mean?

1 What does 'Scat cat!' mean (line 1)?

2 What has the cat done? How do we know?

3 What does 'Drat cat!' mean (line 5)?

4 What does 'Brat cat!' mean? What is a brat (line 9)?

5 What does 'slaughter' mean? Why is it a 'bore' (line 12)?

6 What does 'you live by your law/ and know no other way' mean (lines 16-17)?

7 The poem says the cat is not just a pet. What else is it?

8 Why does the poet say 'welcome back cat!' in the last verse?

9 Is the word 'purr-fect' a real word (line 27)? What does it mean?

10 Do you think the cat will try to kill sparrows again? Why?

Thinking about forgiving

Key question: What does it mean to forgive?

1 In the poem the poet forgave the cat for killing the bird. Why was the cat forgiven?

2 What does forgiving someone mean?

3 Have you ever forgiven someone for doing something you did not like? Explain.

4 Has anyone ever forgiven you for doing something wrong? What happened?

5 When should people be forgiven for doing something wrong?

6 Should you always say sorry for what you have done wrong?

7 Should people always be forgiven whenever they do something wrong?

8 Should you always forgive your friends when they do something wrong?

9 Do you find it easy or hard to forgive someone who has done something wrong?

10 If you forgive someone should you forget what happened? Why or why not?

Further activities

* Find and discuss the use of exclamation marks. Think and write some exclamations.

* Brainstorm all the words that rhyme with 'cat'.

* Discuss and write some instructions on 'How to look after a cat'.

* Read and discuss a story of forgiveness eg The Prodigal Son (Luke 15).

* Write or tell about a time when you forgave somebody or were forgiven.

18
The Blind Boy

O say, what is this thing called light,
   Which I can ne'er enjoy?
What is the blessing of the sight?
   O tell your poor blind boy!

5   You talk of wondrous things you see,
   You say the sun shines bright;
I feel him warm, but how can he
   Then make it day or night?

My day or night myself I make
10   Whene'er I sleep or play;
And could I ever keep awake
   With me 'twere always day.

With heavy sighs I often hear
   You mourn my hapless woe,
15   But sure with patience I may bear
   A loss I ne'er can know.

Then let not what I cannot have
   My cheer of mind destroy;
Whilst thus I sing, I am a king,
20   Although a poor blind boy.

Colley Cibber (1671-1757)

Thinking about the poem

Key question: What does the poem mean?

1   Why cannot the boy see 'this thing called light' (line 1)?

2   What does it mean to be blind?

3   Who do you think talks to him 'of wondrous things you see' (line 5)?

4   What does he want to find out about the sun?

5   Why would it always be day if he could 'ever keep awake' (line 11)?

6   What does it mean, 'you mourn my hapless woe' (line 14)?

7   Who mourns his hapless woe? How does he know this?

8   Why does he bear his blindness with patience?

9   Why can he never know his loss?

10   Why does he think he is a king 'although a poor blind boy' (last line)?

Thinking about seeing

Key question: What does it mean to see?

1   How is it that you can see things? What do you use to see with?

2   Can everyone see? What do we call people who cannot see?

3   Do you know of anyone who is blind? What do you know about them?

4   If you were blind, what would you miss seeing most of all?

5   What could you still do if you were blind? What would be hard to do?

6   Can you know what it would be like to be blind? How?

7   Why are some people blind (eg blind from birth, through accidents, or disease)?

8   How can you tell if someone is blind? How can you help someone who is blind?

9   Can you see something that is not there? Explain.

10   Can you see things in your 'mind's eye'? What does 'I see' mean?

Further activities

- Ask children to put into their own words what the blind boy is thinking in each verse.

- This poem contains some old-fashioned words. What are they? What do they mean?

- Discuss the punctuation in the poem. Where do the sentences begin and end?

- Play seeing and visual memory games eg Kim's Game (*Games for Thinking* in this series, pp 131-144).

- Blindfold a child, see what mystery objects (and people) they can recognise by feel.

19

The Door

Go and open the door.
  Maybe outside there's
  a tree, or a wood,
  a garden,
5   or a magic city.

Go and open the door.
  Maybe a dog's rummaging.
  Maybe you'll see a face,
  or an eye,
10   or the picture
              of a picture.

Go and open the door.
  If there's a fog
  it will clear.

15 Go and open the door.
  Even if there's only
  the darkness ticking,
  even if there's only
  the hollow wind,
20   even if
        nothing
            is there,
go and open the door.

At least
25 there'll be
  a draught.

Miroslav Holub

Thinking about the poem

Key question: What does the poem mean?

1 Who is saying 'Go and open the door' (line 1)?

2 Where or what might this door be?

3 What could a 'magic city' be (line 5)?

4 What would a dog be doing if it was 'rummaging' (line 7)?

5 Whose face or eye might you see outside the door (lines 8/9)?

6 What is a fog? Why will it clear (lines 13/14)?

7 What does 'the darkness ticking' mean (line 17)?

8 What is 'the hollow wind' (line 19)?

9 What does the end of the poem mean 'At least there'll be a draught'?

10 If you opened the door what might you see?

Thinking about finding out

Key question: How do you find out?

1 Have you ever opened a door and been surprised by what you saw?

2 Have you ever wanted to look behind a door which you could not open?

3 Is it always possible to open a door? Why or why not?

4 If you wanted to look behind a door which you could not open, what would you do?

5 Why do people want to open doors and see what is there?

6 If you wanted to know something which you did not know, what would you do?

7 What things can you find out for yourself? Is it good to find out for yourself? Why?

8 What do you need other people to help you find out? Who helps you find things out?

9 Is it possible to find out everything there was to be found out?

10 Are there some things which you will never find out?

Further activities

- Ask children to say what things the poem says that might be outside the door.

- Ask each child to finish the sentence 'Go and open the door, maybe outside there's ...'

- Ask children to find all the words that are repeated in the poem.

- With a folded piece of card with a flap cut out of it, draw a door that opens to show a surprise behind it.

- Ask children to close their eyes and visualise what they might see behind a door.

20

The Frog

Be kind and tender to the Frog,
   And do not call him names,
As 'Slimy skin' or 'Polly-wog',
   Or likewise 'Ugly James',
5 Or 'Gap-a-grin', or 'Toad-gone-wrong',
   Or 'Billy bandy-knees';
The Frog is justly sensitive
   To epithets like these.
No animal will more repay
10   A treatment kind and fair;
At least so lonely people say
who keep a frog (and, by the way,
They are extremely rare).

Hilaire Belloc

Thinking about the poem

Key question: What does the poem mean ?

1 What does it mean to be 'kind and tender' to a frog (line 1)?

2 Why, or why not, should you be kind and tender to a frog?

3 Why might you want to call a frog by a name?

4 Can you remember the names the poem says you should not call a frog?

5 Which do you think is the worst or funniest name to call a frog? Why?

6 Can you think of any other funny names not to call a frog?

7 What do you think 'epithets' might be (line 8)?

8 Why do you think the poem says lonely people might keep a frog?

9 What are extremely rare (last line)? Do you think they are they rare? Why?

10 What should you call a frog?

Thinking about calling names

Key question: Why is what you call someone important?

1 Do you think your name belongs to you? Why?

2 Does a name you call someone say something about them?

3 Are there some names that are unkind to call someone? Can you think of an example?

4 If you want to call someone something, what name should you use? Why?

5 If you want to call someone and don't know their name, what would you call them? Why?

6 Does everyone have their own name? Does everything have a name?

7 Could you give the name Frog to a frog? What name would you call a frog? Why?

8 If you were an alligator and someone called you a rude name, what would you want to do?

9 Has someone ever called you a bad name? Can words or names make you feel bad?

10 Why do people call other people rude names? Should they do it? Why?

Further activities

• Ask children to learn and say a line each, then try to repeat the whole poem a line at a time.

• Discuss made-up names eg 'bandy-knees' (and use of the hyphen). Invent some more.

• Invent some sentences beginning; 'Be kind and tender to the -, and do not -'.

• Find out where each child's name comes from and what it means.

• Write an A-Z of real names or made-up names.

21

The Key to the Kingdom

This is the key to the kingdom.
In that kingdom there is a city.
In that city there is a town.
In that town there is a street.
5   In that street there is a lane.
In that lane there is a yard.
In that yard there is a house.
In that house there is a room.
In that room there is a bed.
10   On that bed there is a basket.
In that basket there are some flowers.
Flower in the basket.
Basket on the bed.
Bed in the room.
15   Room in the house.
House in the yard.
Yard in the lane.
Lane in the street.
Street in the town.
20   Town in the city.
City in the kingdom.
Of that kingdom this is the key.

Anon

Thinking about the poem

Key question: What does the poem mean?

1 What is a kingdom (line 1)?

2 Do we live in a kingdom?

3 What is a city (line 2)?

4 How is a city different from a town?

5 What is a lane (line 5)?

6 What is the difference between a street and a lane?

7 What is a yard (line 6)? What is in the yard?

8 What does the poem say is in the room?

9 Is the poem about one place or many places? (Is it a real kingdom?)

10 What could 'the key' be (first and last line)?

Thinking about places

Key question: Where are we?

1 Where do you live? Do you know your address?

2 Do you have a place that is yours in the house or flat where you live?

3 Do you have something special in a room in your house or flat? What is it? Where is it?

4 Can you describe exactly where your room is, and where your house or flat is?

5 What other places are important in your life? Can you say where they are?

6 If you did not know where you were, how could you find out?

7 Could you be in two places at the same time? Why, or why not?

8 Can you be in no place at all? How, or why?

9 Some places are real, some are imaginary. Where is an imaginary place?

10 Where do you find imaginary places? Can you describe an imaginary place?

Further activities

• Ask children to try to remember all the places from 'key' to 'flowers' and back again.

• Find words beginning with 'b', 'c', 'f', 'h', 'l', 'r', 's', 't', and 'y'.

• Use phrases from the poem for children to turn into sentences eg 'In that town there is ...'

• On a large map show where each child lives.

• Make a book or frieze, illustrating each line of the poem.

22

The Music I Hear

The music is sad
like someone crying
who lost what they had
or a seagull dying
5 singing a last song.

The music is glad
like someone laughing
who found what they lost
or a seagull flying
singing its first song.

The music is slow
like the steps of an old man
who has nowhere to go
and knows nothing other than
10 who he is.

The music is fast
like a marching young man
who has somewhere to go
and knows all that he needs
will be there.

The music is dark
it does not glow with gold,
it has no spark
its sound is cold
15 to the ear.

The music is light
it glows like gold
it has bright sparks
its sound is hot
to the heart.

The music is low
it sounds far away
like the soft fall of snow
on a winter evening
20 as the day ends.

The music is high
it sounds so close
like the warmth of the sun
on a summer morning
as the day begins.

Robert Fisher

Thinking about the poem

Key question: What does the poem mean?

1   What does 'sad' mean? What does the poem say sad music is like (verse 1)?

2   What does 'glad' mean? What does the poem say glad music is like (verse1)?

3   What is 'slow' music? What does the poem say slow music is like (verse 2)?

4   What does 'fast' mean? What does the poem say fast music is like (verse 2)?

5   What does 'dark' mean? What does the poem say dark music is like (verse 3)?

6   What does 'light' mean? What does the poem say light music is like (verse 3)?

7   What does 'low' mean? What does the poem say low music is like (verse 4)?

8   What does 'high' mean? What does the poem say high music is like (verse 4)?

9   Do you think the poem is about one, or more than one piece of music?

10   Is this one poem or two poems? What makes it a poem?

Thinking about listening

Key question: 'What can you hear?'

1   Listen, then tell me, what can you hear?

2   Is there always something to hear?

3   Sounds that we don't like we call noises. What sounds don't you like to hear?

4   What sounds do you like to hear?

5   Some sounds we like are called music. What is music? What is not music?

6   What is your favourite music. Why do you like it?

7   What music do you not like? Why do you not like it?

8   Not all people can hear; some people are deaf. What is it like do you think to be deaf?

9   Hearing is one of your five senses. Do you know what the others are?

10   Which of your senses do you think is most important? Why?

Further activities

• Discuss what is the same or different in the two poems, which they prefer and why.

• List all the opposites (antonyms) in the poems eg slow/fast, and brainstorm more.

• Listen to music and collect words and phrases from children that describe the music.

• See if children can identify different recorded musical and non-musical sounds.

• Go on a listening walk. Note all the sounds that you and the children can hear.

23

The Rescue

The wind is loud,
The wind is blowing,
The waves are big,
The waves are growing.
5   What's that? What's that?
A dog is crying,
It's in the sea,
A dog is crying.
His or hers
10   Or yours or mine?
A dog is crying,
A dog is crying.

Is no-one there?
A boat is going,
15   The waves are big,
A man is rowing,
The waves are big,
The waves are growing.
Where's the dog?
20   It isn't crying
His or hers
Or yours or mine?
Is it dying?
Is it dying?

25   The wind is loud,
The wind is blowing,
The waves are big,
The waves are growing.
Where's the boat?
30   It's upside down.
And where's the dog,
And must it drown?

His or hers
Or yours or mine?
35   O, must it drown,
O, must it drown?

Where's the man?
He's on the sand,
So tired and wet
40   He cannot stand.
And where's the dog?
It's in his hand,
He lays it down
Upon the sand.
45   His or hers
Or yours or mine?
The dog is mine,
The dog is mine!

So tired and wet
50   And still it lies.
I stroke its head,
It opens its eyes,
It wags its tail,
So tired and wet.
55   I call its name,
For its my pet,
Not his or hers
Or yours, but mine -
And up it gets,
60   And up it gets!

Ian Seraillier

Thinking about the poem

Key question: What does the poem mean?

1   Where does the rescue take place?

2   What is the weather like?

3   What is the sea like?

4   Who is writing the poem?

5   What does the poet hear?

6   What does the poet see in the water?

7   What does the poet feel when he says 'O must it drown?' (line 31)?

8   What does it mean to drown?

9   How is the dog rescued?

10   What is special about the dog?

Thinking about pets

Key question: What is a pet?

1   Do you have any pets at home? Describe your pet.

2   If you could have any animal for a pet which would you choose? Say why.

3   What animal could you not have as a pet at home? Say why.

4   What is a pet?

5   Can only animals be pets? Could you have a pet toy? Explain why.

6   Can people be pets? Explain why.

7   What should you do to care for your pet? Why should you?

8   People often love their pets. Do you think pets love their owners?

9   Would you like to be a pet? Which pet animal would you choose to be? Why?

10   What is the difference between an animal and a human being?

Further activities

• Ask children to close their eyes to try to visualise events while you read the poem.

• Ask children to retell the story slowly, while you sketch in cartoon form what they describe.

• Identify the questions in the poem, hide the poem and record questions they remember.

• Invite children and other pet owners to talk and record how they care for their pets.

• Read and discuss more poems about pets (see anthology *Pet Poems, ed.* R. Fisher, Faber).

24

The Tree in Season

Spring
The tree hums quietly to itself
a lullaby to the birds
bursting with baby leaves
5   and in all its new green glory
the tree begins to sing

Summer
The tree stretches in the sun
it knows the birds that fly
10   the beasts that run, climb and jump
from its heavy loaded branches
it yawns and digs its roots
deep into the still centre
of the spinning earth

15   *Autumn*
The tree shivers in the shortening day
its leaves turn gold
the clouds pass
the seeds fall
20   the tree drops its coins of gold
and the days are rich
with the spending of leaves

Winter
Old branches ache
25   the tree stands naked in the storm
frozen bleak and bare
deep underground life lies sleeping
the tree sleeps
and waits for the returning sun
30   to wake him
from his woody dreams

Robert Fisher

Thinking about the poem

Key question: What does the poem mean?

1   What does it mean 'The tree hums quietly to itself' (verse 1)?

2   What is the 'new green glory' of the tree in spring (verse 1)?

3   What happens to the tree in the poem in summer (verse 2)?

4   What is 'the still centre of the spinning earth' (verse 2)?

5   What changes happen to the tree in the poem in autumn (verse 3)?

6   What does it mean 'the days are rich with the spending of leaves' (verse 3)?

7   What happens to the tree in winter (verse 4)?

8   What 'woody dreams' do you think a tree might have (last line)?

9   Why is the poem called 'The tree in season'? What is a season?

10 How is a tree similar to, and different from, a person like you or me?

Thinking about changes

Key question: What changes?

1   What things change in your life?

2   What things do not change in your life?

3   Are some changes good? Are some changes bad? Give examples.

4   Does everything in nature change?

5   What can you see that is different today from yesterday?

6   What changes take place that you cannot see?

7   What changes would you like to see in this room?

8   What changes would you like to happen in your life?

9   What changes would you like to see happen in the world?

10 How could you help make something change for the better?

Further activities

- Discuss which verse of the poem children like best, or least, and why.

- Brainstorm all the words children can think of to do with trees.

- Children complete their own sentence beginning 'The –...' eg 'The sky...' for each season.

- Illustrate how a tree changes in spring, summer, autumn and winter.

- Study a range of pictures and photos and ask children to sort them into seasonal categories. Discuss.

25

The Wee Wee Woman

A wee wee woman
lived in a wee wee house.
One night in bed
she heard a wee wee noise.
5   She crept out of bed
and lit her wee wee candle.
She looked under her wee wee table.
She looked under her wee wee chair.
There was nothing there.
10   She blew out her wee wee candle;
and went back to her wee wee bed.
The wee wee woman closed her eyes.
Then she heard a noise!
She crept out of bed
15   and lit her wee wee candle.
She looked under her wee wee table.
She looked under her wee wee chair.
There was nothing there.
She blew out her wee wee candle,
20   and went back to her wee wee bed.
The wee wee woman closed her eyes.
Then she heard a noise!
She crept out of bed
and lit her wee wee candle.
25   She crept downstairs
to her wee wee table, she lifted the cloth
and had a wee wee peek,
and out popped – BOO!
'Well well,' said the woman,
30   'Think of that!
To be frightened of nothing
but boo!'

Anon

Thinking about the poem

Key question: What does the poem mean?

1   What does 'wee wee' mean in the title 'The *Wee Wee* Woman?

2   When does the poem take place? How do you know?

3   Was the woman in the house alone?

4   What sort of noise do you think she heard?

5   Where did she look, and what did she find the first time she got out of bed?

6   How many times did she hear the noise?

7   What did she do the second time she got out of bed?

8   What popped out from under the cloth on the table?

9   What do you think the 'BOO!' was? Did she see it or hear it? Was it real?

10   Was she really frightened of nothing?

Thinking about being afraid

Key question: What is there to fear?

1   Have you ever been afraid of something? Explain.

2   Have you ever been afraid of something that turned out to be nothing to be afraid of?

3   Are you afraid of the dark? Why?

4   What happens when you are afraid (eg shiver, bite nails, chatter, have goosebumps)?

5   Some people fear spiders, thunder, or the dentist. What are you most afraid of?

6   Have you ever made someone else feel afraid?

7   How can you stop feeling afraid (eg sing, talk to yourself, talk to others)?

8   Does everyone feel afraid sometimes?

9   Fear is a feeling. What other *feelings* do we all have?

10   When is it sensible to feel afraid? When is it not sensible to feel afraid?

Further activities

• Ask children to tell the story of the poem as if they were the wee wee woman.

• Find the exclamation 'BOO!' Think of other sound-words. Write them as exclamations.

• Make up sentences using as many words beginning with 'w' as possible.

• Tell or write a story about hearing noises in the night.

• Discuss poems about fear, eg 'I Once Dressed Up' and 'The Voice in the Tunnel' from *Ghosts Galore* ed R. Fisher (Faber).

26
When it is Time

When it is time to party
and you receive your present
remember those children
who are given nothing.

5   When it is time to play
and your friends are waiting
remember those children
with none to share their dreams.

When it is time to eat
10   of your favourite food
remember those children
who go hungry to bed.

When you are thirsty for drink
and it is there when you want it
15   *remember* those children
whose wells have no water.

When it is time for school
and you do not want to go
remember those children
20   who have nowhere to learn.

When it is time to go home
and you think home is dull
remember those children
who have nowhere called home.

Robert Fisher

Thinking about the poem

Key question: What does the poem mean?

1 What kind of party might be meant in the first line?

2 Why might some children be given nothing (line 4)?

3 When is it time to play with friends (lines 5/6)? What might you play?

4 What does it mean 'those children with none to share their dreams' (line 8)?

5 Why might some children 'go hungry to bed' (line12)?

6 What does it mean 'those children whose wells have no water' (lines 15/16)?

7 Why might some children 'have nowhere to learn' (line 20)?

8 Why might you think home was 'dull' (line 22)?

9 Why might some children 'have nowhere to call home' (last line)?

10 Why does the poet say we should we remember these children?

Thinking about others

Key question: Why should we think of others?

1 Could you live on your own with no other people in the world? How, or why?

2 Who are the important people in your life? Why are they important?

3 If other people do things for us, should we do anything for them? Why?

4 Do you have friends? How do you make someone your friend?

5 Can a friend be someone you do not like or who does not like you?

6 How do your friends know that you like them?

7 Can people be happy without friends?

8 Should you be selfish, or share things with others? Why?

9 Do you know someone who has felt unhappy? How could you help them?

10 How could you help people who are starving or who have no homes to live in?

Further activities

- Say the first two lines of each verse and ask children to recall the last two lines.

- Discuss the syllable sounds in the word 'remember' and syllable sounds in other words.

- Ask children to finish their own sentences beginning 'When it is time to ...'

- Find out from a children's charity about children in need. Discuss how you could help.

- Create a poster of a child in need with a caption beginning 'Remember ...'

27
Where Are They Now?

He was a rat, and she was a rat,
    And down in one hole they did dwell,
And both were as black as a witch's cat,
    And they loved one another well.

5   He had a tail, and she had a tail,
    Both long and curling and fine;
And each said, 'Yours is the finest tail
    In the world, excepting mine.'

He smelt the cheese, and she smelt the cheese,
10   And they both pronounced it good;
And both remarked it would greatly add
    To the charms of their daily food.

So he ventured out, and she ventured out,
    And I saw them go with pain;
15 But what befell them I never can tell,
    For they never came back again.

Anon

The Cats of Kilkenny

There was once two cats of Kilkenny,
Each thought there was one cat too many;
So they fought and they fit,
And they scratched and they bit.
5   Till, excepting their nails
And the tips of their tails,
Instead of two cats there weren't any!

Anon

Thinking about the poems

Key question: What does the poem mean?

1   When it says of the rats 'down in a hole they did dwell,' what does 'dwell' mean (line 2)?
2   Where might the hole have been? Why did they live there?
3   When it says 'they loved on another well' (line 4) what does this mean?
4   Why did each say 'Yours is the finest tail in the world , excepting mine' (line 8)?
5   Where might the cheese have been that they smelt (line 9)?
6   What do you think their daily food was (line 12)?
7   What does 'venture' mean (line 13)? Why did they venture out?
8   Who 'saw them go with pain'? Why was it a pain to see them go out?
9   What happened? Why do you think they never came back again (poem 1, last line)?
10 What do you think happened to the cats of Kilkenny?

Thinking about mysteries

Key question: What is a mystery?

1   Do you know everything? Why not?
2   Do you think anyone knows everything?
3   Tell me one thing you do not know.
4   If you don't know something, how can you find out?
5   What is a mystery? (If no-one knows the answer to a question, it is called a mystery.)
6   Do you know of any mysteries?
7   Have you ever had anything that just seemed to disappear?
8   What is the strangest thing you have ever seen? Was it a mystery?
9   What is the strangest story you have ever heard? Was it a mystery?
10 Is the world a mystery? Why or why not?

Further activities

* Re-read the poem, with you and the children adding actions in mime.
* Ask the children to think of a question to ask the rats.
* Find alternative rhyming words for words at the end of each line.
* Write and tell what surprising thing might have happened to the rats.
* Read about a real mystery such as the Loch Ness monster (see *First Stories for Thinking*, p 74) or the Marie Celeste (*Stories for Thinking*, p 78).

28
Who Can Tell the Time?

In the forest
the old owl hoots.
'Who can tell the time?'
Above the trees
5   the moon looks down.
'What can we see of time?'
In grass below
is a mouse that dreams.
'What is now the time?'
10   There is no sound
but the cuckoo's song.
'What do we hear of time?'
The forest path
is all overgrown.
15   *'If time is lost can time be found?'*
The stars appear, the stars are gone.
The forest sleeps, the forest wakes.
'What do we know of time?'

Robert Fisher

Will there really be a 'Morning'?

Will there really be a 'Morning'?
Is there such a thing as 'Day'?
Could I see it from the mountains
If I were as tall as they?

5   Has it feet like Water lilies?
Has it feathers like a Bird?
Is it brought from famous countries
Of which one has never heard?

Oh, some scholar! Oh, some sailor!
10   Oh, some wise man from the skies!
Please to tell a little Pilgrim
Where the place called 'Morning' lies!

Emily Dickinson

Thinking about the poems

Key question: What does the poem mean?

1 What in the forest does the old owl hoot? What word does an owl's hoot sound like?

2 Who can tell the time (line 3)? Can you? Can anything in the forest?

3 What can we see of time (line 6)?

4 What could the mouse be dreaming of (line 8)?

5 It says 'there is no sound but the cuckoo's song' (lines 10/11). What sounds might there be?

6 When do stars appear or go (line 16)? When does the forest sleep or wake (line 17)?

7 Who is asking the questions in the poem (poem 1 or poem 2)?

8 What is a 'Morning'? What is a 'Day' (poem 2, line 1)?

9 What questions does the poet ask (poem 1 or poem 2)?

10 Who is the poet talking to?

Thinking about time

Key question: What is time?'

1 Who can tell the time?

2 Do you know what the time is? Is it the same time in every place?

3 What does three *o'clock* mean?

4 What is an hour, a minute, a second?

5 If clocks stop, does time stop? Why?

6 If there were no clocks or watches would there be no time? Why?

7 How long have you lived (how old are you)? How do you know how old you are?

8 What is a year, a month, a day?

9 Can time go backwards? Could you grow younger every day? Why?

10 Does time ever seem to go faster or slower? Why?

Further activities

- Using a clock, ask the children what might be happening in a forest during each hour.

- Ask children to complete the sentence 'In the forest ...'

- Identify the questions and question marks in the poems. Make up questions about time.

- Illustrate a timeline to show what happens during a day, a week, a month or a year.

- Study ways of telling time eg clocks, stopwatch, sundials, calendars, diaries, timetables.

29

Witches' Spell

Double, double, toil and trouble;
Fire burn, and cauldron bubble.
Fillet of fenny snake
In the cauldron boil and bake;
5 Eye of newt, and toe of frog,
Wool of bat, and tongue of dog,
Adder's fork, and blind worm's sting,
Lizard's leg and owlet's wing –
For a charm of powerful trouble,
10 Like a hell-broth, boil and bubble.
Double, double, toil and trouble;
Fire burn, and cauldron bubble.

William Shakespeare, Macbeth

Thinking about the poem

Key question: What does the poem mean?

1 This poem is said by three witches in a play by William Shakespeare. What is a witch?
2 These words said by the witches are called a 'spell'. What is a spell?
3 What do you think the witches are doing as they say this spell?
4 What is a cauldron?
5 What sort of things are they putting in the cauldron?
6 How do you think they make the fire to heat the cauldron?
7 What do you think a 'charm' is (line 9)?
8 What powerful trouble do you think they might be trying to cause (line 9)?
9 Why do they call it a 'hell-broth' (line 10)? What does each word mean?
10 Why do they say 'Double double, toil and trouble'?

Thinking about magic

Key question: What is magic?

1 Were the witches trying to do magic?
2 Do you think magic spells work? Why?
3 Do you think there are witches or wizards who can do magic?
4 Is trying to make magic good or bad?
5 Are witches or wizards good or bad?
6 Have you ever seen someone do a magic trick? Was it really magic?
7 Have you ever tried to do something that was magic?
8 What makes something 'magic'?
9 Do you know any stories about magic? Give an example. Could the story be true?
10 If you could do one piece of magic what would it be? Why do you want to do it?

Further activities

- Ask the children to describe the witches and the scene.
- Chant the poem, pointing to the words, then add actions and sound effects.
- Look for alliterative phrases eg 'Double double, toil and trouble'. Make up your own.
- Write and illustrate your own magic spells.
- Read more poems about witches and spells eg *Witch Words* ed. R. Fisher (Faber).

30
Why?

Why is grass always green?
What holds up the sky?
Why is hair upon my head?
Why, oh why, oh why?

5 Why does rain go down, not up?
Why is salt in every sea?
Why is there a sun and moon?
Why is there only one me?

Why do bees buzz and birds sing?
10 Why do nails grow on my toes?
How long is a piece of string?
Why is it no-one knows?

Why is night so full of dreams?
Why do we have one nose, two eyes?
15 Why do questions never end?
Why are there so many whys?

Robert Fisher

Thinking about the poem

Key question: What does the poem mean?

1   What is the title of this poem?

2   Why does the poem have that title?

3   How many verses does the poem have?

4   How many questions are there in the poem?

5   Can you answer any of the questions in the poem?

6   What question in the poem do you think is hardest to answer?

7   Why is the question 'How long is a piece of string?' hard to answer?

8   Can you see any words that rhyme?

9   Why is this called a poem?

10   Do you like this poem? Why, or why not?

Thinking about questions

Key question: What is a question?

1   What is a question?

2   Why do people ask questions?

3   Who asks you questions? Can you remember a question you have been asked?

4   Do you ask yourself questions? Can you remember a question you have asked yourself?

5   Do you ask other people questions? Give an example.

6   Do people always know the answer to your questions? Why, or why not?

7   Do you always know the answer? Does anyone know all the answers? (If so, who?)

8   Is it good to ask questions? Why, or why not?

9   Is it ever wrong to ask a question? If so, when or why?

10   If you want to find out something what can you do? How else can you find out?

Further activities

• Ask the children if there is anything they do not understand about the poem.

• Write on board children's questions or comments on the poem to discuss.

• Make a class list of words that rhyme with words in the poem eg why/my.

• Ask children to make up a list, or poem, of their own questions to share with others.

• Have a Question Hunt. Children look in books to see how many questions they can find, or how many question-marks there are in a piece of text.

Glossary of terms

acrostic poem	A poem in which the initial letters of each line make a word or words when read downwards.
alliteration	The repetition of initial letters in words either next to or near to each other, as in 'makes much of a miracle'.
anthology	A collection of poems or passages of writing, often with a unifying theme.
assonance	The repetition of similar vowel sounds close to each other, to achieve a particular kind of word music or rhyme.
ballad	A poem or song which tells a story. The traditional ballad was an anonymous folk ballad characterised by short verses and simple words. Literary ballads were written in the 19th and 20th centuries, such as Tennyson's 'Lady of Shallott'. The word ballad today also refers to songs of love.
blank verse	Poetry written in *iambic pentameters* (five stress lines), without rhymes. Most of Shakespeare's plays are written in blank verse.
carol	A form of song often sung at Christmas which originated in France as a kind of round dance.
cinquain	A poetic form invented by American poet Adelaide Crapsey with the following syllabic line count: 2, 4, 6, 8, 2.
cliché	Language that has become stale and commonplace through repetition.
collage poem	A poem that has been put together from lines, sentences or phrases from other sources.
consonance	The repetition of the same consonant in words close to each other.
couplet	Two adjacent lines of the same metre which rhyme.
dialect	A way of speaking or writing that is special to a locality or social group.
draft	A rough plan, outline or working version of a piece of writing.
elegy	A sad poem or lament about the death of a particular person.
epic	A long poem, usually about a heroic adventure. Traditional epics include *Beowulf*, and the *Iliad* and *Odyssey* of Homer.
epigram	A short, neat and often witty saying.
epitaph	An inscription that is or could be written on a tombstone.
eye rhyme	A pair of syllables which look as though they should rhyme but do not, for example 'love' and 'move'.
fantasy	Strange, imaginative and non-realistic kinds of thinking or writing.
first person	Speaking or writing using the 'I' voice.

form or format	The physical appearance of a poem on the page in terms of size or line arrangement. Poems are either free form and could be written down in different ways, or are fixed form such as *sonnet, cinquain*, and *villanelle*.
found poem	A poem that has not been deliberately composed but has been found by chance in another context, for example as part of an advert.
free association	A spontaneous connecting of images and ideas.
free verse	Poetry that does not use a traditional rhyming pattern.
haiku	Originally a short Japanese poem of three lines with the syllabic count of 5, 7, 5 and with the first and third lines rhyming.
half-rhyme	A rhyme that does not rhyme fully, but only partially eg 'Beanz meanz - Heinz.'
iambic pentameter	A line with five stressed syllables. English poets have used the iambic line for poetry since the time of Chaucer. Most ballads, songs, hymns and poems have been written in it.
imagery	Vivid description of a visible object or scene so that we can see or sense what is being written about.
kenning	An Old English poetic convention in which one object is represented by another which is associated with it, for example 'whale's road' meaning 'sea'.
limerick	A comic or nonsense poem writen in five lines, using the rhyming scheme AABBA, in which the third and fourth lines are shorter than the rest.
lyric	Originally in Greek 'of the lyre'. Later used about any short poem which expresses a strong feeling or mood. Now used to refer to the words of a song.
metaphor	A type of figurative language in which one thing is described in terms of another thing eg 'All the world's a stage'. Metaphors, since Aristotle, have been seen as the most distinctive type of poetic language. A whole poem can be an extended metaphor.
metre	Means 'measure', and refers to the regular rhythms of stressed and unstressed syllables in poetry.
narrative poem	A poem that tells a story or narrates a series of events.
nonsense verse	Verse that for funny or playful reasons does not make obvious sense.
ode	A poem expressing strong feeling that is longer and more complex than a lyric.
onomatopoeia	A word whose sound imitates its meaning eg dong, ping, whizz, zoom.
oral tradition	Traditional stories, songs and poems handed down by word of mouth from one generation to another.
palindrome	A poem or sentence which reads the same backwards or forwards.
parable	A short story or poem which has a hidden moral or spiritual meaning.
parody	To imitate a piece of writing, usually to make fun of the original.
pastoral	A form of writing derived from ancient Greek and Latin literature in which the countryside and its people are celebrated.
personification	Presenting an object or idea as a person with human qualities or feelings.
prose poem	Writing written as prose but with the sound quality and compression of poetry.

quatrain	The most common stanza in English poetry, consisting of four lines, usually rhymed.
rap	Rhythmic spoken poetry, sometimes set to music, which probably originated in street carnivals in the West Indies.
refrain	A phrase or verse which recurs at intervals, especially at the end of each stanza of a poem or song.
renga	A series of *haiku* linked by a common theme.
rhyme	Words or final syllables in words which sound identical or very similar, usually occurring at the ends of lines of verse. A rhyme may be one syllable (house/mouse), two syllable (looking/cooking) or three syllables (bicycle/tricycle). A rhyme scheme is the pattern of rhyming sounds that occur in a poem. These are usually indicated by letters of the alphabet eg ABAB.
rhythm	The pattern of stressed and unstressed syllables in speech. In poetry the rhythmic unit is called the metre or measure.
run-on line	Lines in which the meaning and syntax lead you on to the next line eg 'It's funny how the things you're told/Can never lead to pots of gold.'
scansion	The analysis of the metrical pattern of a poem.
shape poem	A poem written in the shape of an object.
simile	The direct comparison of one thing with another, generally connected with 'as' or 'like' eg 'pure as a pearl'.
sonnet	A fixed form of poem, generally fourteen lines, using iambic pentameter (five stresses per line).
stanza	The group of lines in which a poem is divided.
stress	That part of a word or syllable on which the emphasis falls when spoken. Stress can be loudness, raised pitch or length of syllable. Stress is a feature of all English speech. In poetry it creates rhythm.
surreal	Something which seems dreamlike or absurd.
syllable	The smallest unit of English speech sound (phoneme). A syllable must include a central vowel (some words like 'I', 'a' and 'oh' contain no more than this). Some words are one syllable eg 'tree' and others are multisyllabic. The way syllables are stressed or unstressed creates the rhythms of speech and poetry. Some poems such as haiku and cinquains have a set number of syllables.
symbol	A particular type of sign where an object represents another object, relationship or idea, for example a dove may represent peace.
theme	The main idea of a poem, or what the poem is about. A poem may have a number of themes.
tone	The attitude suggested by the voice of the poem eg humorous, sad, lonely, gentle, angry.
villanelle	A fixed form of poem, containing 19 lines, with five three-line stanzas and a final four line stanza.

Acknowledgements

We are grateful for permission to use the following copyright material:

'The Colours' from *Hailstones and Halibut Bones* by Mary O'Neill and Leonard Weisgard, III. Copyright © 1961 by Mary Leduc O'Neill. Used by permission of Doubleday, a division of Random House, Inc. 'Daddy Fell into the Pond' by Alfred Noyes, from *Collected Poems*, published by John Murray (Publishers) Ltd. 'The Frog' by Hilaire Belloc, reprinted by permission of the Peters Fraser and Dunlop Group Limited on behalf of the estate of Hilaire Belloc. 'Public Speaking' by Sandra Willingham, by permission of Ginn and Company Ltd. 'Emma Hackett's Newsbook' from *Please Mrs Butler* by Allan Alhberg (Kestrel, 1983). Copyright © Allan Alhberg, 1983. 'Fairy Story' by Stevie Smith from *The Collected Poems of Stevie Smith* (Penguin 20th Century Classics), by permission of James MacGibbon. 'The Rescue' by Ian Serraillier, by permission of Anne Seraillier.

Acknowledgments are also made to any copyright holder whom the author has been unable to trace in spite of careful inquiry.